I'M GOING TO BE
BAPTIZED

I'M GOING TO BE
BAPTIZED

SUSAN EVANS McCLOUD

Bookcraft
Salt Lake City, Utah

ISBN O-88494-512-X

First printing, 1983

Cover art and interior illustrations by Vicki Jacobson.

Lithographed in the United States of America
PUBLISHERS PRESS
Salt Lake City, Utah

To Jared James Grant McCloud, "My Bonnie Lad," and to Rachel Beth Briggs, "Racin' Rachel."

Chapter One

The late spring sun was pale, but it felt warm on Jared's head as he walked along Fourth South. Kitty-corner across the street stood the junior high school, and, even from this distance, Jared could recognize several of his friends among the boys who jumped and hollered and stretched to catch the ball. The boy at bat hit a high left-fielder that arched to the edge of the baseball diamond. Jared watched it hit and disappear somewhere in the straggly bushes along the sidewalk.

It was Sunday afternoon, and Jared wasn't out to play ball. He had told Adam, his best friend, in Sunday School that morning that he guessed he wouldn't see him at the game. Adam always asked him if he was going to play with the guys on Sunday, and Jared always told him no. But that never seemed to make any difference to Adam. Jared didn't play on Sunday because that's what his parents had taught him—that you keep the Sabbath day holy, that you only do certain, special things on the Lord's day. And now that he was nearly eight it wasn't even hard for Jared to say no. It was what he wanted to do himself, without anyone having to tell him that it was the right thing to do.

Jared was on his way home from running an errand for his mother. She had sent him with a pie and a loaf of homemade bread to Sister Briggs who lived three blocks away. Sister Briggs was sick again, and Jared's mother was worried. And the reason she sent Jared and not one of his older brothers or sisters was because Rachel Briggs was Jared's age. And, even though she was a girl, Jared liked her a lot, and his mother knew it, and so she knew that Jared would be the perfect one to take the pie and bread.

Now he was at the corner, and he could have turned and gone the long way home to avoid the boys, but it was too late. Billy Jones had already spotted him. He and Dennis Adams were hollering to him with their hands cupped around their mouths, and there was no way Jared could walk around the corner and ignore them now.

So he crossed the street to the junior high. He walked slowly, with his hands stuck in his pockets and his eyes looking everywhere but at the group of boys on the field. Jared wasn't afraid, exactly. He liked to fight, and he knew there wasn't a boy there he'd be scared to wrestle with. But Jared hated having someone make fun of him. And he knew that was exactly what would happen if he refused to enter the game.

Sure enough, as soon as Jim Jensen had shown Jared his new cub scout pocket knife and Tom Long had bragged about the five stitches in his leg from where he rode his bike into a fence, Dennis asked Jared if he'd stay and join the game; they could sure use a good pitcher. And when Jared said no—he'd like to, but he couldn't—the guys just kind of stood there. But Matthew Williams leaned on his bat and laughed and said, "Jared's afraid his daddy will give him a lickin' if he stays." A few of the boys laughed at that.

"Or maybe he's afraid he'll get all dirty and be late for Church," Matthew taunted. He just wouldn't shut up.

Finally Jared had to turn his back and walk off, with the sound of Matthew's laughter following him. He felt his face burning, and he realized that his hands in his pockets were tightened into fists. He tried to relax. He tried to not hate Matthew Williams. Jared forced himself to think of the words of the song which had always helped him so much in the past.

Dare to do right . . . dare to be true,
You have a work that no other can do;
Do it so bravely, so kindly, so well,
Angels will hasten the story to tell.
Dare . . . dare . . . dare to do right!

Jared liked those words. They made him feel strong and happy inside. Besides, he could imagine his grandfather watching him. Grandpa Davis had died last winter, and Jared missed him. He missed sitting on the old man's knee and listening to stories of the days when there were no space ships or televisions or drive-in movies. Days when boys who lived on a farm woke up at five in the morning to help with the chores, and the only time a boy tasted candy was at Christmas . . . if he was lucky.

Grandpa Davis had always told him, "A man makes his own freedom. The Lord has given us the tools to work with, but every man decides for himself just which things will bind him and which will not." Here he would pause and stroke his moustache, and his bright blue eyes would seem to pierce through Jared so that he trembled and tingled inside.

"Remember, boy, the chains you drag through life will be of your own making. And nothing can bind them so tightly around a man as ignorance, selfishness, and pride. Those three are dangerous, Jared, so watch out for them. Ignorance, selfishness, and pride."

Jared loved Grandpa Davis. It just seemed right, somehow, that the old man would be looking out for him, even though they couldn't see each other and talk to each other anymore.

Jared picked up a stick and threw it wide, loving the feel of his own arm as it curved into the air. It was funny, but he felt free inside, somehow. He wished Grandpa Davis could see him now. The saddest thing about having him gone was that the old man wouldn't be there when Jared was baptized in May. Whenever he pictured it in his mind, Jared had always imagined his grandpa there, standing in the confirmation circle with his hands on Jared's head.

Jared had waited so long to become a member of the Church. He was number six, the last in the family. Now all his brothers and sisters were baptized except him. His oldest brother, Jacob, was on a mission in Australia, and Todd was twelve and had the priesthood. Jared was the only one who wasn't "official" yet. It was the hardest thing he had ever waited for in his life.

He turned the corner onto Lincoln Street, and he could see his own house three doors down. His mother would have dinner ready, and he knew his big sister, Sarah, had baked a chocolate cake for dessert. Jared broke into a run. He counted off the seconds it took him as he cut across the lawns, cleared the stairs, and burst inside his own front door.

Chapter Two

School the next day seemed long and hot, and it was difficult for Jared to hold still. As soon as the bell rang, he was out the door, and in no time at all he had run the block and a half to his house. He changed into old clothes, because he knew he was going to get dirty. He grabbed a thick slice of cheese, then ran to meet Adam at their secret place in the alley half a block from Jared's house.

Adam was already there when Jared arrived. He was busy dragging piles of weeds and loose branches to the spot they had discovered, where they were going to build their hut.

Adam looked up when he saw Jared and grinned. Jared broke off a piece of cheese and handed it to Adam. Then together they worked, dragging boards and the old cushions Adam had brought from home until their hut was cozy and protected, with a hole just big enough to crawl through for an entrance, and a shelf in the back where the two boys could set their treasures.

"I'll bring my wasp nest and my jar of black widow eggs," Jared promised Adam. "Maybe Todd will let me bring the old cow skull Uncle John gave him last summer. It's just stuck back in the garage somewhere. He doesn't care about it anymore."

"I'll bet he'll let you have it then!" Adam was excited. He stretched out on the floor of the hut, his hands folded behind his head. "This is going to be the neatest hut in the world, Jared. Neater than the one Kenny Cole and his gang built last summer. I wish they could see us now!"

Jared stretched out beside Adam and closed his eyes. He could smell the damp earth and crushed leaves, but it didn't smell like dirt, it smelled rich and clean. And as hard as Jared listened, he couldn't hear any cars or any voices. He felt as though he had been swallowed into another world, where no one else existed. There was no sound here except the secret, rustling noises of tiny insects and animals he couldn't even see, and the sudden brittle whirring of a grasshopper, so close that the sound seemed to be coming from inside Jared's own head.

Before Jared and Adam left the hut they checked to make sure no one else was around, so there wouldn't be any chance of someone seeing them. And they promised to bring their treasures the next day after school. And their guns and holsters, too, just in case there was trouble.

Jared was so dirty he had to take a bath before dinner. And after dinner and the dishes and the chores were done, it was home night, with everybody together. Jared liked home night—the songs and the lessons and the silly games they played, laughing and feeling happy together.

Tonight the lesson was on free agency. Jared's father explained that agency is the ability and the freedom to choose either good or evil. His sister, Sally, had made a chart of the four principles which must be there if agency is to exist. She asked Jared to read the chart out loud. Everyone in the family knew how much Jared loved to read out loud. And everyone knew how good he was at it, even when the words were long ones and difficult to pronounce.

"Law," he read, as the first principle listed on the chart. "There have to be laws to be either obeyed or disobeyed."

They talked about that a minute and named some of the laws Heavenly Father has given His children: to love God above all else, to love your neighbor as yourself, to not steal or lie, to keep the Sabbath day holy . . . on and on the list went. Jared hadn't realized before how many there were!

At last it was time for the second point, and Jared read out loud: "Opposites. The law of opposites must exist: good and evil, sin and right-eousness, misery and joy." Jared knew enough about that one, you could bet! It seemed he always felt these two forces pulling against each other inside him. He knew there were times when right won the battle, like Sunday at the junior high when he chose the right and stuck to it, in spite of Matthew's taunts. But things didn't always work out that well.

Todd was nudging him in the ribs, and Jared realized it was time to read the third principle listed on Sally's chart. "A knowledge of good and evil," Jared read. Heavenly Father had certainly filled His part of the bargain as far as knowledge was concerned! There was the *Bible*, the *Book of Mormon*, and the *Doctrine and Covenants* and *Pearl of Great Price* given to Joseph Smith during the early days of the Church. And there was a living prophet today, who still spoke with Jesus and received revelations to guide everyone who was in the Church.

At last Jared read the fourth principle from the chart: "An unfettered power of choice." He had to ask about that one. He had never realized before how much power he had over his own life. Jared decided it was really the same thing as Grandpa Davis always told him when he was alive, "A man makes his own freedom. The Lord has given us the tools to work with, but every man decides for himself just which things will bind him and which will not." Grandpa Davis had understood it all along. And he sure had a fancy ways of putting it into words!

After two helpings of rhubarb cake with warm rhubarb sauce spread on top, Jared excused himself from the table. Before his mother could tell him it was time for bed, he slipped outside. There was a tall old elm tree in Jared's back yard with a little wooden seat built all the way around the trunk. Jared sat there and gazed up at the sky, feeling lonely and a little sad.

He was wishing he had a dog. A dog of his very own. Maybe then he wouldn't feel so lonely. But the family had a dog already. An old black Labrador who was older than Jared himself. But the Lab was mostly Todd's dog, anyway, or nobody's dog at all. For as long as he could remember, Jared had wanted a dog, a dog that would be his, and his alone.

He felt something soft brush his arm and looked up to see his mother's face close to his.

"What are you thinking about?" she asked him.

"I don't know," he said. "I was wishing I had a dog. And before that I was feeling sort of lonely and wondering why it's so hard sometimes to do what's right."

"What things do you have the most trouble with, Jared?" his mother asked him.

He didn't have to think about that one. He knew what things he had trouble with, all right.

"The trouble is," he blurted out, "I like to fight. I'm not mean to little kids or anything like that, but I like to fight. And sometimes I don't tell the truth. And I don't always obey you, and I tease Sarah and Sally and Beth, even when they ask me not to. I'm not good enough to be baptized, and I don't

9

know if I ever will be."

"It's good that you can recognize your faults, Jared, and that you want to do something about them. I'll help you and so will your father. And so will someone else."

"Who is the someone else?" Jared asked her.

"Your Father in heaven. Remember, he knew you before. He knew all that was strong and beautiful about you. And He trusted you to come down to earth and learn all the truths you have forgotten and live those truths so well that you'll be able to return to him again."

That sounded exciting to Jared. He liked the idea of proving himself, of overcoming hardships, of doing wonderful things! He could imagine how proud his Grandpa Davis would be when Jared met him again. Maybe it would be something like that with Heavenly Father, too.

He leaned back against his mother and closed his eyes. The night breeze blew cool on his face, the crickets played their music in the grass, and Jared felt very happy inside.

Chapter Three

The next afternoon Jared loaded his treasures carefully into an old card-board box. Sure enough, Todd had given him the cow skull! That went into the box first. Then he put in his wasp nest, the jar of black widow eggs, his two bird's nests, and some of the nicest rocks and petrified wood he had collected. His cap gun was carefully strapped at his side, and Jared walked as quickly as he could down the long dusty alley toward the secret hut.

The heavy box bumped against his legs, but he never stopped to put it down and rest. He was too anxious to get to the hut and arrange his treasures. He could already imagine how perfect it all would look! At last he saw the thick bank of lilac bushes off to his right. He put the box down carefully at his feet and straightened up to look around him. As soon as he saw Adam come out from behind the bushes he knew that something must be wrong.

"It's gone, Jared. Somebody's wrecked the hut!"

"What the heck!" Jared was beside his friend in an instant. It was true. The hut they had built so carefully and been so proud of was a total wreck. Even the cushions had been cut and slashed, their stuffing scattered among the weeds and bushes. As he looked at the mess before him, something hard began to grow inside Jared—something hard and hot and

angry.

"Matthew Williams," he said, and he looked up so that his eyes met Adam's. Adam nodded.

"You bet. What are we going to do about it?"

Jared didn't even have to think. "Let's go get him," he said, and the hard angry feeling surged through him so that he couldn't even hold still.

But they didn't get him. When Jared and Adam found Matthew Williams he was at the elementary school grounds riding bikes with his big brother and his brother's friends. And he was too much of a coward to admit what he had done.

"What old hut? You mean that mess behind the bushes in the alley, with a bunch of cushions and dirty boards? I never touched any old hut."

Then he laughed at Jared and Adam, did a wheelie on his bike, and rode off with his brother and his brother's friends. Jared was so frustrated that he wanted to cry. There was nothing left to do but drag his box of treasures home again and stuff them back into the shed.

When he walked into the house, he was hot and dirty. Without really meaning to he blurted out all of the anger and frustration he was feeling inside.

"Matthew Williams wrecked our hut. He's a liar and a coward. If I could get my hands on him, I'd give him the beating of his life."

Jared stood in the middle of the kitchen floor, so angry and defiant that none of his older brothers or sisters even laughed. But his father got up from the chair he was sitting in. He put his hands on Jared's shoulders and gently led him out of the room.

When they were alone together, he said, "I've been meaning to talk to you about Matthew Williams, Jared. He's . . ."

"There's nothing to talk about," Jared interrupted. "He's a mean, lying coward. I wish he would just drop dead somewhere and leave me alone!"

Jared's father knit his brow, and his eyes held that serious, no-nonsense look Jared knew so well.

"I think you'd better settle down, Jared," he said. "That's no way for a boy who's about to get baptized to talk."

Suddenly it all came back. Last night under the stars with his mother. Who he was . . . and why he was here . . . and all the grand and glorious things he was going to do to make his Heavenly Father proud of him. How could he have forgotten them all so quickly? How could he feel so mean and angry inside? Jared felt hot tears stinging his eyes, and he wiped them away impatiently. Long, dirty tear streaks stained his cheeks.

His father put his hand on Jared's shoulder.

"Jared," he said, and his voice was low and warm. "I don't think I realized before what a hard time you've been having. I didn't know Matthew was

13

such a trial for you. Perhaps what I want to ask you will be too difficult for you to do."

In spite of himself, Jared was immediately curious. "What? What did you want me to do?"

"Well, actually, Jared, I need your help with something I've been worried about for a long time."

His father paused. What, Jared wondered, could his father be talking about?

"You know, Jared, that I'm one of the home teachers for Matthew's family. And so I know there are some problems Matthew's father and mother are struggling with. Because of these problems they are sometimes very unhappy—and so is Matthew. And because of some of these problems Matthew hasn't been baptized yet, even though he turned eight nearly four months ago."

Jared's eyes grew big as he listened to his father talk. Matthew came to Sunday School and Primary only once in awhile, and when Jared thought of the boys and girls he knew who were members of the Church, he didn't even count Matthew Williams. He hadn't realized that Matthew had already turned eight and that he hadn't been baptized.

"I don't think Matthew wants to be baptized," Jared said to his father. "He never acts like he does."

"Oh, but sometimes we can't tell what people think and feel by the way they act," his father answered. Jared knew he was right, because he remembered how easy it was for him to act mean or angry when he was feeling sad or frightened inside, when he was wishing all the time that he could be patient and good and kind.

"You see, Jared," his father continued, "I have come to love the Williams family. I'm concerned about them. I want to help them. I was wondering if you would want to help me . . . if you could, somehow, want to help Matthew Williams, too."

"I don't know," Jared answered, and he felt his heart thumping against his chest as he thought of the idea. "It would sure be a hard thing to do."

"I know it would, Jared. But *I* know you could do it. I know what a blessing it would be to you—how strong and happy it would make you feel. You're preparing yourself to be baptized into the Church and obey the commandments of your Heavenly Father, Jared. Don't you think you might as well begin right now?"

Jared didn't answer. He thought it was an awfully big thing his father was asking him to do.

Chapter Four

"Do you know what some of the covenants are that you make when you enter the waters of baptism?" his father asked.

Jared shook his head no, so his father continued.

"You covenant, or promise, to come into the Church, or the kingdom of God, to be numbered among His people, and to take upon you the name of Christ. Taking upon you the name of Christ means you will try to be like Him."

"I know," Jared said eagerly. "I know that's what you and mother are always trying to do. You've told us lots of times that Jesus is the example our whole family is trying to live up to."

"That's right, Jared. Even parents aren't perfect. But as we work on our faults, we grow stronger and better each day."

"What are some of the other things I will promise when I get baptized?" Jared asked.

"You will promise to love and help others, Jared. And to serve your Heavenly Father by keeping His commandments."

"So I should start by trying to love Matthew Williams." Jared's voice was very little, and he looked down at his feet as he spoke.

"It isn't hard to love those who love you, Jared. Your parents, your brothers and sisters, your best friend who loves you and is kind to you. The Savior loved those who hated and persecuted him. So did the Prophet Joseph Smith. So have all great men who have lived throughout the history of the world. Wouldn't you like to be one of them?"

Jared looked up at his father. If only his father knew how much Jared wanted to be that kind of a man!

"Your Heavenly Father has blessed you, Jared. He's given you many things to make your life happy, to help you be strong and good. Do you think you could share some of those things with someone who needs them?"

Jared had never thought of Matthew Williams as needing anything! He always seemed so cocky and sure of himself. Then he remembered something. His mother always told him that people who were mean or unkind usually behaved that way because they were scared or unhappy inside. Could it be that Matthew Williams was really scared and unhappy inside?

Jared thought about last night with his mother. He thought about his brother, Jacob, who was on a mission loving people and sharing with people he had never seen before. He thought about his Grandpa Davis.

"All right," he told his father. "I'll do it. I'll try to help and love Matthew Williams, if it's the last thing I do!"

Jared's father smiled. "Remember, Jared, your Heavenly Father will help you. It is His work you are doing, and you can count on Him to help you each step of the way. Remember when you pray to tell Him how you feel and to really ask Him for His help."

Jared shuffled his feet and looked down again. "But I'm only a kid."

"And you don't think Heavenly Father will pay much attention to your prayers?" his father asked. "You should know better than that, Jared. Don't you remember the stories of Samuel, of David, of the children who prayed for the Prophet Joseph Smith?"

Jared did remember! He thought of the story of the children who heard that Joseph Smith was in danger from his enemies. Because they loved him so well, they knelt down together and asked Heavenly Father to protect him.

Their mother heard them praying and went to the Prophet. When he learned of the children's love and faith, he turned to his friends who had gathered to help and protect him and said, "Go to your homes. There will be no need of your help. Heavenly Father has heard the prayer of the children, and no harm will come to me tonight."

Could he have the kind of faith and power those children had? He sat down on the couch beside his father, and they talked for a long time, planning things Jared could do to help Matthew Williams.

Chapter Five

The air was warm. Jared felt the back of his shirt sticking against his skin. He took a deep breath and ran a little faster. He was jogging around the school with his class. Three times around the school made a mile, and Jared had just one long side of the playground left to go.

Suddenly he felt a sharp pain as an elbow jabbed into his left side and another pain in the shin of his left leg. He stumbled, barely regaining his balance as Matthew ran past him, grinning from ear to ear.

"Stop hoggin' the road, Jared. You slow runners ought to keep to the right and let the rest of us guys past."

Jared knew Matthew was only on his second lap of the school. Jared knew he could run faster than Matthew and fight harder than Matthew. But what difference did that make? Jared had promised that he would help Matthew Williams and be patient and kind no matter what Matthew did.

Jared dropped down in the shade at the edge of the playground. As hard as he had expected it to be, he had never known it would be as bad as this! He felt so dumb every time he was nice to Matthew. It just seemed to give Matthew and his friends more opportunities to make fun of Jared and pester him. It was nearly two weeks now since Jared had first talked with his father. And, in spite of all his trying, nothing seemed any different.

Nothing seemed any better than before. Jared got up with a sigh and walked back into the classroom.

Later that afternoon when school was out, Jared headed for the rack where his bicycle was locked up with the rest. Dennis and Billy and a couple of other guys were gathered there. As he got closer, he realized they were waiting for him. They cleared a path for him, and Billy kicked the back tire on Jared's bike.

"Deader 'n a doornail," he said, as Jared bent down to look. "Front tire, too."

"Jared," Tom Long broke in, "I saw Matthew Williams and his big brother hangin' around here at recess."

"It sure looks suspicious," Dennis agreed. He bent down by Jared to run his hand over the flabby, wrinkled tire that hung from the rim of Jared's wheel. Jared straightened himself up.

"Thanks, guys," he said and started undoing the combination lock that held his bike to the rack.

"Whadda ya gonna do?" Billy demanded.

"Go home and fix my bike, I guess. Todd will help me."

Jared paused, then wheeled his bike out onto the playground. He knew

his friends thought something was wrong with him. He knew they expected him to be angry and ready to go out and get Matthew Williams. But how could he explain to them what he was trying to do?

He said good-bye and began wheeling his bike across the warm blacktop, the tires thump-thumping in dull little thuds. They sounded just like Jared felt—dull and tired and numb inside.

As he reached the sidewalk, Jared nearly bumped right into Rachel, who was standing there watching him. She started walking along beside him, even though her own house was in the other direction.

"What's going on, Jared? Why are you so nice to Matthew Williams lately? He's meaner than ever to you."

Jared felt his face go warm and his ears burn. Rachel had noticed. Rachel, of all people, and he could tell she thought he was some kind of a dummy! He looked down and watched the tire as it wobbled along the cement.

"I don't know. I just feel like it, I guess."

"You just feel like it?" Rachel was indignant. "You just feel like being nice to Matthew—all of a sudden—when he's meaner to you than ever before!"

It was easy to tell that Rachel didn't swallow that answer at all. Jared stopped his bike and looked at Rachel. Her brown eyes were serious and intent, and the little brown freckles seemed to dance across her face as she wrinkled her nose at him.

"Okay, Rachel, I'll tell you. But I wouldn't tell anyone else. And you've got to promise not to tell a single, living soul."

Rachel promised, her eyes bright. So Jared told her about the talk he had with his father and the things he had promised to do. He told her how hard he had been working and praying and, as he talked, he felt strong and brave and good inside.

"Gee whiz," Rachel said, "that's really something. I don't know how you do it, Jared."

Jared had never felt so good before. Just knowing that Rachel knew and understood would make it so much easier from now on. He wheeled his bike across the street, and Rachel walked beside him, saying

nothing. When they reached the sidewalk, she said, "Jared." And her voice sounded funny and a little scared. "Would you like some help? I mean, would you like it . . . well, if you don't mind . . ."

Rachel was having a hard time. Jared stopped his bike and waited for her. Finally she said, "I'm getting baptized in May, too, you know. If you'd like, I'll help you try to be nice to Matthew. Maybe if there were two of us working at once . . ."

"Gosh, Rachel!" Jared had never been so excited. "Do you mean it? Would you really? It would be great if you would!"

They talked all the way to the next corner, when Rachel had to turn to walk to her own house. Jared watched her go, wishing he could tell her, somehow, what a big difference she had made. He had been so tired of trying, so discouraged before. But now, with Rachel's help . . .

Rachel walked home slowly. She was thinking about some of the things

Jared had told her. She was the oldest child in her family. Her father had told her more than once that her little brother and sisters looked up to her and tried to be like her. It gave her a warm feeling inside, and she wanted to be a good example.

But sometimes it was hard. Especially when her mother was sick and Rachel had so many extra things to do around the house. Then she would begin to feel sorry for herself and yell at her little sister and say no when her baby brother wanted her to read to him. And every time she acted that way she felt miserable and unhappy inside.

And now, with her own baptism only a few weeks away, Jared had given her a perfect opportunity. If she worked hard and was patient and kind to Matthew Williams, and said her prayers every single night, then surely she could be nice to her own little brother and sisters whom she loved so much! Rachel was excited. She whistled the last block home, thinking about how happy her mother would be and wondering what her father would say when he noticed how kind and patient and happy she was going to be.

Chapter Six

It *was* easier for Jared after that. It was as if he and Rachel had a secret conspiracy, and no matter what Matthew Williams did or said, *they* knew something *he* didn't know! So Jared would just be nice and smile at Matthew, and, if Rachel was there, she would smile, too, so that the freckles crinkled across her nose, and Jared wanted to laugh out loud. Sometimes Matthew would get a funny look on his face, like he wondered what was going on. Then Jared knew they were getting through to him at last.

Jared's father told him it would take time before Matthew would trust Jared and believe that he really meant to be kind, that he really wanted to be friends. So Jared kept praying and trying. And he was so grateful to Rachel that he bought a special model of an old-fashioned car and built it for Rachel's birthday. Jared loved to make models, and he worked on this one with special attention and care so that even Todd thought it was one of the sharpest models he had ever seen. Rachel loved it, and she invited Jared over to take turns riding on her uncle's big Harley-Davidson motor-cycle. Rachel was one of the prettiest, most-feminine girls Jared knew. But he sure was glad that she liked guns and cars and baseball and motorcycles, too!

The Sunday after Rachel's birthday Jared's class had a lesson on baptism. Jared liked his teacher, even though she put her arm around Jared's shoulder on the way to class and embarrassed him by talking about how he and Rachel and Dennis were going to be baptized at the end of the month.

Jared tried to listen carefully as she talked about how baptism began with Adam when the earth was young and new. She said whenever the Lord had a people on the earth, then baptism would be found among them. She reminded the class that Jesus, himself, set an example for all of us when He was baptized.

Rachel was so smart, Jared thought. It seemed she answered all the questions. She knew that Jesus was baptized in the River Jordan by John the Baptist, who loved Jesus, and didn't feel worthy to baptize him. But Jesus said it must be done "to fulfill all righteousness." In every thing He taught us and set us a perfect example that we could follow safely, knowing that it was right and true, because Jesus had given it to us.

When his teacher told about the part she called the Apostasy, it made Jared feel sad inside. She explained how Jesus completed His mission and went back to live with his Father in Heaven again. And He left His work

on earth in the hands of His helpers, the Twelve Apostles whom He had ordained, giving them the power they needed to continue His work.

But there were wicked men who didn't want to see the Apostles do the work Jesus had left them. These men fought against the Apostles and persecuted the members of Christ's church, until many people had been killed. After even the Apostles were killed by the wicked men, Heavenly Father took His Church away from the earth, and with it His authority, because men were too unrighteous to have the truth and take care of it the way Heavenly Father wanted them to do. And so the correct form of baptism was lost, and the power to baptize no longer was found among men.

Jared couldn't help wondering how Jesus must have felt when He saw what the wicked men were doing, after He had worked so hard and suffered so much to bring His truth to the earth. At first he thought that Jesus must have been very angry, but then he remembered what his father had told him about how Jesus loved those who hated and persecuted Him—just as Jared was trying to love Matthew Williams. And he realized that Jesus didn't hate the wicked people; He loved them and felt sorry for them instead.

26

After Sunday School Rachel came up to Jared. She was carrying two copies of the picture their teacher had given them. It was a picture of Jesus with the scripture written underneath:

"And whoso believeth in me, and is baptized, the same shall be saved; and they are they who shall inherit the kingdom of God." (3 Nephi 12:33)

"Let's take one to Matthew," Rachel said. Jared had never once, in all the long weeks he had been working on Matthew, gone near the Williams' house. He hated to admit it, but he was a little scared of the idea of going there and maybe seeing Matthew's father and mother and not knowing what to do or say. But how could he tell Rachel he was afraid?

So he walked with her to the Williams' house. He hoped no one would come to the door when he rang the bell. But the door opened right away. Sister Williams looked a little surprised as she asked them what they wanted. Sure enough, Matthew was home, out in the back yard playing with his dog. Jared and Rachel walked back together. Jared had never felt more foolish. But Rachel walked right up to Matthew and handed him the picture.

"We got these in Sunday School today. Jared and I thought you might like one, so we brought it over."

Matthew was surprised.

"What is it?" he said, as he took the picture from Rachel's hand. Rachel nudged Jared in the ribs, as though she expected him to have an answer all ready.

"It's a picture of Jesus," Jared said, though he could barely get his voice to come out of his throat. "We had a pretty good lesson about Jesus and baptism and the Apostles and all that."

"I don't need any old lessons about Jesus," Matthew said. Then Rachel surprised Jared, and Matthew, too.

"Yes, you do," she said. "Jared and Dennis and I are getting baptized the end of May, and we wish you could get baptized with us, don't we, Jared?"

Jared couldn't believe it! "You bet," he said. "It's gonna be pretty special, and we'd sure like it if you could be baptized, too."

27

"So you ought to learn a little bit about Jesus first, don't you think?"

Rachel asked it so prettily that Matthew didn't know what to reply. They all just stood there a moment, looking at each other.

"Well, we'd better get going," Jared said. "We just wanted you to know we missed you today."

"That's right," Rachel said. "We hope you can come next week, Matthew. Bye, see you at school."

Somehow they got out the back gate and down the driveway and away from the house. Jared was trembling inside, and his hands were sweaty. Rachel smiled at him, her eyes shining.

"That was easier than I thought it would be," she said.

Jared wasn't sure he agreed.

"I'll bet Matthew will sure have something to say tomorrow. Me and you coming together to invite him to Sunday School! We'll never hear the end of it!"

"I don't care what he does. I feel good inside," Rachel said, "and I won't let him ruin that!"

Matthew stood still in the middle of the yard after Rachel and Jared left. He stared down at the picture in his hands. He walked over to the garbage cans to throw it away, but then he stopped. No one else was around to see him. So he slipped into the house, got out his mother's tape, and stuck the picture on the wall above his bed.

Chapter Seven

There wasn't enough room. The shed was crowded with junk, everything piled topsy turvy on top of everything else. And his father had asked Jared to clean it up! He didn't even know where to begin.

He kicked at an old tire that lay by his feet, feeling sorry for himself. He looked up at the shelf filled with jars and nests, rocks and cocoons—his own things that should be arranged neatly in his own secret hut. But, thanks to Matthew Williams, they were piled with all the rest of the junk in his father's shed. And thanks to Matthew Williams, Jared wasn't even looking forward to his own eighth birthday party that he had waited for so long.

As he worked on the shed, he thought about it. His birthday party was only three days away. Yesterday afternoon he had taken invitations around to his friends. And he had taken one to Matthew's house. Jared had thought about it for a long time and prayed about it night after night. He knew this was what he had to do. Matthew had shown up in Sunday School last week for the first time in months. And he wasn't teasing Jared as much or being quite the smart aleck he had been before. That was real progress, and Jared knew he could spoil it all if he left Matthew out of his party.

After he had made his decision and was addressing the invitations, his

father came into the room. He thumbed through the envelopes, glancing at the names, and when he came to Matthew's, he stopped. He looked as though he didn't quite know what to say. He put his hand on Jared's shoulder and said, "I'm proud of you, Jared. You're really quite a boy."

So Jared knew how happy his father was. He tried to be happy, too. But he was worried. He didn't want to have to look out for Matthew at his own party. He didn't want anything awful to happen. He didn't want his own eighth birthday party spoiled because of Matthew Williams!

By now he had dragged all the junk out of the shed. It was bigger than he had thought in there. He stood looking it over a moment. He couldn't help thinking what a perfect house it would make for a dog. Even Matthew had a dog. Jared was feeling sorry for himself again, and he knew it. He grabbed the broom and attacked the inside of the shed with such energy that billows of dust spilled out into the bright spring air.

When Jared's birthday finally did arrive, he was too excited to worry about anything, even Matthew Williams. His father and his older brother, Todd, were taking Jared and his friends go-cart riding, and Jared could hardly wait! As the boys piled into the car to drive to the go-cart track, Jared made sure that he smiled at Matthew, but Matthew didn't smile back. He looked kind of stiff. If Jared hadn't known better, he might have thought Matthew looked just a little bit afraid.

When they reached the track, the boys piled out, racing each other to reach what they thought looked like the meanest, fastest car. Jared slid into the low, hard seat and stretched his legs out in front of him. He could smell oil and old rubber and gasoline, and he loved it! He gripped the steering wheel, found the gas pedal with his foot, and waited for the signal from the man in the greasy coveralls that they could begin the race.

There were six boys all lined up and crowded together. When the man waved his hand, Tom Long and Jared were the first to shoot out into the track. Around one wide curve they drove, neck to neck, with Adam and Dennis right behind. The next curve was tight, but Jared slid into the inside slot, barely missing the stacks of piled up tires that marked the boundaries and lined the road. That gave him an advantage, and he pulled out ahead of Tom until they had covered the track four times, and the race was over, and Jared had won!

He was so excited that he couldn't help grinning from ear to ear! The boys were all laughing and talking together, challenging each other before the next race. Then Jared noticed that Matthew wasn't saying anything, and no one seemed to be paying him much attention.

Jared thought suddenly, "Matthew doesn't really belong in a group like this. He doesn't know how to act or what to do if he can't be bullying some kid, then riding off on his five-speed bike."

So Jared watched Matthew during the next race, and maybe because of that, he only came in second. But he discovered that Matthew didn't know anything about driving a go-cart. He would wobble and swerve all over the track, blocking the other boys so that they hollered at him to get out of the way. And he was always hitting the stacked tires along the edge with the corner of his bumper, so that he would bounce back onto the track, then slow down again, trying to regain some control of his car. At first the thought popped into Jared's mind: "It serves him right, for once!" But he couldn't help feeling sorry for Matthew. Jared could tell how uncomfortable he was. Matthew kept rubbing his hands nervously down his pants legs. His eyes kept looking from place to place, as if he didn't care, or didn't even notice, that no one was paying attention to him.

The cars lined up for the third and last race. Jared knew he could win! Two wins out of three and he would be the unquestioned champion. The man gave the signal, and Jared started off.

For awhile Adam and Dennis were right beside him. Once or twice Dennis pulled ahead, but on the corners Jared always made up speed and came into a new stretch in the lead.

Then, as he approached the far end of the track, Jared watched with amazement as Matthew, who had been going faster than usual on the straight, open track, seemed to lose control of his car and bolt off the road. With a crash and a thud he landed in the tires. The fat black tires scattered and bounced in every direction. Matthew's car, the tires screeching, turned all the way around twice, stopping with a jolt in the dirt at the side of the track.

It looked like Matthew wasn't hurt, but Jared couldn't really tell. He still had time to slow down and help him, but if he did, he would lose the race for sure. Yet, maybe, if he stopped, Matthew would believe at last that Jared really did want to be his friend.

33

He slowed his car and pulled off beside Matthew, trying to ignore the sharp pain he felt inside as he watched Dennis and Adam fly past. Jared got out of his car and walked over to Matthew.

"You all right?" he asked.

"Yeah," Matthew answered, but his voice was all mumbled, and he wouldn't look up at Jared. "That was sure a dumb thing to do. I don't know how it happened. I . . ."

"Aw, don't worry about it," Jared said, and he put his hand on Matthew's shoulder. "It takes awhile to get the knack of these things. Have you ever driven a go-cart before?"

Matthew shook his head.

"Well, you see, I've been coming out here with my big brothers ever since I can remember. It's pretty easy for me by now."

"I made you lose the race," Matthew mumbled, still not looking up. "Why'd you stop?"

"Because I wanted to," Jared answered. And he knew, as he said it, that he really meant it this time. "I wanted to make sure you were okay."

Jared paused, feeling suddenly awkward. But Matthew had looked up, his face smudged with sweat and dirt.

"Thanks, Jared," he said. "Thanks a lot."

Jared didn't know what to reply. His heart was thumping against his chest. He grinned at Matthew and helped him straighten his car. Then they drove up the track to join the rest of the boys. And when they reached the group, nobody said a word about Dennis winning the race. But one or two of the guys went up to Matthew and clapped him on the back and asked him how he had survived the big wreck. Jared saw that Matthew was grinning from ear to ear.

Jared could hardly contain his excitement. After the go-carts they stopped for tall, frosty glasses of root beer. The guys were laughing and joking together, but all Jared could think about was the look on Matthew's face when he said, "Thanks, Jared, thanks a lot." And he couldn't believe what a wonderful feeling it had given him.

35

Back at Jared's house he opened the gifts his friends had brought, and they ate big wedges of frosted birthday cake and tall ice cream sundaes. Jared was happy. He had never had a birthday like this before.

After his friends had left and his mother and sisters had cleaned up the dishes and the party mess, Jared's dad asked him to go get his tool box from the shed. Jared pulled open the door, glad he had cleaned the place up, so he knew right where to find the box of tools. But, as soon as he looked inside, he stopped dead. Then he let out the loudest, longest yell he could, dropped down on his knees, and wrapped his arms around the warm, wiggly body of the little puppy who had run to meet him. Jared looked up to see his whole family gathered around him.

"Whadda ya think of her?" Todd asked, his eyes sparkling.

"Isn't she adorable?" Amy crooned, leaning down to pet the puppy's silken head.

"Is she all mine?" Jared hardly dared believe it could be true.

"She's all yours, Jared," his father answered. "You've earned her these past weeks. You've done a lot of growing up, and your mother and I think you'll be able to handle her just fine."

After everyone else got tired of playing with the puppy, Jared held his dog on his lap, whispering silly things into the floppy ear, wondering how it was possible for one boy to hold all the happiness he felt bursting inside him.

Chapter Eight

A few days before Jared's baptism a letter came from his brother, Jacob; the one who was on a mission in Australia. The letter was addressed to Jared, himself. Jared was excited! The whole family gathered together, and Jared read the long letter out loud.

In the letter Jacob said how much he loved Jared and how thrilled he was when he thought about Jared getting baptized. Then he told Jared about some of the people he was baptizing that month.

One was an old man who suffered from arthritis so badly that he could barely walk. He was always in pain, but he was gentle and patient and so happy to be baptized. As he had stood in the font with Jacob, tears of joy had run down his wrinkled cheeks.

Another was a woman who had three small children but no husband. She had to leave her children every day and work to get money to feed and care for them. But she was still poor, and in order to be baptized, she had to travel from the city she lived in to the city where the baptism was being held. This meant missing time at work that she needed and spending what little money she had to make the trip, and staying with strangers when she arrived in the strange city. But she had faith that this was what her Heavenly Father wanted her to do. She knew He would bless her and help her,

somehow, to take care of her little children.

The last person Jacob told about was a young man. He was so excited about the gospel that he read everything Jacob could give him. He had already read the *Book of Mormon* through twice and prayed about it. He knew with all his heart that what he was doing in joining the Church was right. But it was a good thing for the young man that his testimony was so strong, because his family—which was very rich and powerful—was angry at the young man for wanting to become a Mormon. When he told them he was going to join the Church, his father told him not to come home anymore. So the young man went to live with friends, and his family wouldn't talk to him or see him. They wouldn't even answer the letters he wrote. The young man was sad and hurt, but he wasn't discouraged. He felt that what he was suffering wasn't much to give in return for the gospel of Jesus Christ.

Jared saw that there were tears in his mother's eyes when he had finished reading Jacob's letter. He could feel tears in his own eyes, too. These people Jacob wrote about lived on the other side of the world, but they seemed very real to Jared. He felt that he shared something with them, though he wasn't sure how. The gift of baptism . . . that's what Jacob had called it. He shared with them the gift of baptism, given by a loving Father who wanted to bring truth and joy and purpose into the lives of His children everywhere.

Jared thought about Jacob's letter while he was feeding his dog and playing with her in the yard. Jared had named his new puppy Taffy, and he had already taught her to trust him. She would come when he called and sit quietly while Jared buckled the halter around her belly and snapped on the leash to take Taffy for a walk. How Jared loved the bright, gentle little dog!

When he went into the house to wash his hands, Jared's mother was cooking dinner, and no one else was around. So he asked her to tell him about Joseph Smith's baptism, because he couldn't quite remember, and he wanted to know. So, while he stirred the noodles on the stove and chewed on a stalk of celery, his mother told him the story again.

"You remember the lesson your teacher gave you a few weeks ago about the Apostasy?" she asked Jared.

"Yes," he replied, "when people began to change the truth and do wrong things, and Heavenly Father took His power from the earth."

"That's right, Jared," his mother smiled. "You have such a good memory! Well, when Heavenly Father decided it was time for him to give His authority to men again, He needed to restore that authority, didn't He? Return all the rights and keys men would need to act in His name and with His power."

Jared nodded, and his mother went on.

"So that's what He did with the Prophet Joseph Smith. He prepared him a little at a time and gave him truths and powers bit by bit as he was ready for them, until everything had been restored or returned. The power to baptize came when Joseph and Oliver Cowdery were working together on the translation of the *Book of Mormon.*

"As they were reading the book, they came to a part about baptism that they didn't really understand. So, knowing they would receive an answer, they knelt to ask the Lord in prayer."

"How did they know they would receive an answer? Wasn't Joseph afraid that nothing would happen?" Jared asked.

"That's a very good question. But you see, Jared, Joseph Smith had already had so many answers to his questions and his prayers that he knew by this time he could trust the Lord. And with that kind of faith he approached Him.

"The two young men knelt in prayer among the tall, quiet trees, and an angel came to them. He introduced himself as John the Baptist."

Jared's face lit up. "John the Baptist! He baptized Jesus!"

"That's right. And John held the Aaronic Priesthood, which has the power to baptize. He ordained Joseph Smith and Oliver Cowdery to the Aaronic Priesthood. Now they had the power they needed, too. John commanded them to baptize one another. So there, in the beautiful Susquehanna River, Joseph baptized Oliver, then Oliver baptized him. About a month later Jesus' own apostles, Peter, James, and John, came and restored to Joseph the higher, or Melchizedek Priesthood. This priesthood contains other powers and keys. Then Joseph was able to organize on the earth again the true Church of Jesus Christ."

"It's so exciting!" Jared said, his eyes dancing. "I wish I'd have known Joseph Smith. I wish I'd have been there."

"You know, Jared, your own baptism is very exciting when you think about it. John the Baptist over a hundred years ago made it possible for you to be baptized today. And there's another important thing I want you to remember, Jared. The Lord works the same way with all His people as He did with Joseph Smith."

"What do you mean?" Jared asked.

"When you are in need of light and knowledge and pray to the Lord in faith, He will give you the help and the answers you need, just as He did when the Prophet Joseph asked Him."

That seemed like an awfully big promise. Jared wasn't sure.

"Joseph Smith was pretty important. What about me?"

Jared's mother came over and stood beside him. She put her hands on his shoulders and looked down at him with a smile.

"You're pretty important, too, Jared Campbell. What you do and what you become are important to the Lord. He knows you, and He loves you. Don't ever forget that, Jared—not ever in all your life."

"I won't forget," Jared promised.

Chapter Nine

The rain was like a curtain of water, cold and wet. The sky was black, and the trees were black and shiny. Jared shivered as he brushed his hair back with a wet hand. He stood for a long moment outside the shed, not even caring that the rain was dripping down his neck and running from his hair into his eyes. The shed door was open, and Taffy was gone!

A sick, tight feeling started to settle in Jared's stomach. It was impossible! When he first saw the storm clouds gathering, Jared had gone to the shed himself and fed Taffy and latched the door. But now the hook was open, the door stood wide to the wind and rain, and Taffy was gone!

He turned, searching for his dog everywhere, calling her name until his throat hurt, but it was no use. She had disappeared into the dark, angry storm. Discouraged, soaked to the skin, Jared finally went back into the house, fighting the tears that were stinging in his throat. It didn't seem right to be here in the light, warm kitchen when Taffy was lost and afraid out in the storm.

Todd, when he saw Jared, could tell that something was wrong.

"Taffy's gone," Jared told him, as he began to peel off his coat and his wet clothes. "The latch on the shed was unlocked, and Taffy's disappeared."

"How did the shed get unlocked?" asked Jared's sister, Sally, who had walked into the kitchen and heard what he said.

"I'll bet *I* know who unlocked it!" Ten-year-old Beth followed her sister into the room with a smug look on her face.

"What do you mean?" Jared demanded. "What are you talking about?"

"Well," Beth started out, trying to sound important, "I saw Matthew Williams fooling around out there when I went to Cindy's house. He looked mighty suspicious. I asked him what he wanted, but he only mumbled something under his breath and walked away."

Now everyone began talking at once. "Matthew Williams . . . of course!"

"How dare he do such a thing!"

"Well, I wouldn't put it past him."

Finally Jared shouted above the voices, "Wait! Wait, Beth. What time did you go to Cindy's house?"

"Half an hour ago," she answered primly. "I only took over a book she needed and hurried back home."

It was true, then. At least it was true that Matthew Williams *could* have been the one, for it was over an hour since Jared had fed his dog and carefully latched the door.

"What are you going to do, Jared?"

"He ought to be ashamed of himself, treating you like that, after all you've tried to do for him!"

"Some people can never be trusted!"

"Well, Jared, what are you going to do?"

Suddenly Jared realized that everyone was looking at him. They were all angry and ready to condemn Matthew Williams. They all loved Jared and felt sorry for him and were ready to take his side. He looked from face to face carefully. Finally he spoke.

"I don't think Matthew did it."

Instantly everyone began talking again. "You don't think he did it? What do you mean?"

"Of course, Matthew did it. Who else would do a mean thing like that?"

"Beth saw him!"

45

"What else would he be snooping around in our yard for, except to cause some kind of trouble?"

"No," Jared heard himself saying, "I don't believe Matthew would do that kind of thing anymore. He was probably just hanging around wanting to play and afraid to come and ask. I . . . I won't believe he did it! I won't!"

Jared turned and ran out of the kitchen and up to his own bedroom. It was getting dark now, and he could hear the angry clatter of the rain on his window. He pressed his face against the cold glass, but everything looked blurred and dark. He felt miserable inside. What would he do if he lost his dog? Where was Taffy now? Maybe she was lying dead in the street, or wandering through the fields, frightened and crying, her beautiful coat streaked with mud and matted with burrs.

It would be easier if Jared could blame Matthew in his own mind. If he believed that Matthew had let his dog out just for spite, then at least Jared would have someone to be mad at now. But things had changed. The hard, hurting anger he used to feel against Matthew Williams just wouldn't come.

Chapter Ten

When Jared's father came home, he and Jared drove around in the car, back and forth across the neighborhood streets, through the muddy alleys, searching for a wet little shape that might be Taffy. Jared rolled down his window and called and called, until he was hoarse and wet and shivering, but no little shape appeared out of the darkness. No sound found its way above the greedy noises of the storm.

At last his father drove home. When Jared got into the house, he went right up to his bedroom, closed the door, and dropped down on his knees. He tried to tell his Heavenly Father how he felt—how he really felt inside. He tried to have faith that Heavenly Father loved him, that He really cared what happened with Jared and Taffy—that he cared what happened with Matthew Williams, too.

It was nearly nine o'clock, and Jared was all ready for bed, when he heard a loud pounding on the kitchen door. He was at the door in an instant. He flung it open. Standing there on the back porch, muddy and wet all over, was Matthew Williams. And in his arms, shivering and bedraggled, was Taffy!

Without really knowing how it happened, Matthew and Taffy were suddenly indoors, and Taffy was in Jared's arms! Her soaked little body left splotchy stains of mud and rain all over Jared's robe and along the

legs of his pajamas. He grabbed an old towel from under the sink and wrapped Taffy in it. He rubbed her wet coat and talked to her softly to stop her from shivering. Suddenly Jared remembered Matthew!

He looked up to see Matthew standing just inside the kitchen door, a dirty puddle of water at his feet. He looked cold and miserable and uncomfortable. But at Jared's smile his face lit up.

"I found her in the field, Jared. I was driving past on my bike, and when I heard her whining, I knew it was a dog in there!"

For one brief moment a doubt flashed through Jared's mind.

"How could you tell it was a dog, with all the noise from the wind and the rain?"

Matthew didn't know that Jared doubted him, and he couldn't keep a look of pride from creeping over his face.

"Dunno. I'm good at that kind of thing. Ya see, that's how I got my own dog. Found him in an old irrigation ditch one day. My dad said if I cleaned him up and took care of him, I could keep him. Well, anyhow, I crawled back into the bushes, but she was stuck behind some boards and a roll of fencing. She was too scared to move—just huddled back there, making it harder than ever for me to reach her."

"You cut your arm," Jared interrupted, noticing for the first time the long red welts that crisscrossed each other on Matthew's wrist.

"Aw, that's nothing. I didn't know it was your dog 'til I'd almost got her out. But I was sure glad then that I'd found her, that's for sure!"

"So am I! Gee, Matthew, thanks a lot!"

"Aw, that's all right. Guess it gave me a chance to do something for you, after all the things you been doing for me."

Jared didn't know what to say. There was a long, awkward pause when Jared could feel Taffy shivering through the towel and hear the tick of the clock on the kitchen wall. Then suddenly his mother was there, helping Matthew with his wet coat, saying nice things to him, taking care of everything. And, before he knew it, Jared and Matthew were sitting together at the table, drinking hot chocolate and eating some of his sister Sarah's homemade chocolate chip cookies. And his mother didn't say anything about the puddles on the floor or the muddy stains on Jared's robe.

After three cups of hot chocolate, Matthew pushed back his chair. "Well, I guess I'd better get home," he said.

Jared stood up and got Matthew's coat. It had dried some since his mother had hung it over the heater.

49

"Thanks again, Matthew."

"Aw, that's okay," Matthew answered. "See ya Saturday, Jared."

"Saturday?" Jared didn't know what Matthew meant.

"The baptism," Matthew answered, a grin on his face. "My dad said I could get baptized with the rest of you on Saturday. Had my interview with the bishop last night. My Grandpa Williams is gonna baptize me, I guess."

Jared was elated. "Matthew, that's great! Wait till I tell Rachel!"

"Rachel?" It was Matthew's turn to be surprised. And Jared was so embarrassed he wished he could disappear into one of the muddy puddles on the floor.

"Rachel's been concerned about you, Matthew. She'll be happy to learn that you're going to be baptized. We're all happy for you, Matthew."

It was Jared's mother's voice. She had come to his rescue! And she had never sounded so sweet to Jared before.

"Thanks," Matthew mumbled. He was a little embarrassed himself now. He pulled on his jacket and was out the back door in no time at all.

"See you Saturday," Jared called, and the two boys grinned at each other before Matthew disappeared into the drizzling rain.

Chapter Eleven

At last the day for Jared's baptism was here! He couldn't believe that he was going to be honestly, officially baptized into the Church at last.

All the necessary steps had been taken. Jared and his parents had met with the bishop, and the bishop had talked with him about the importance and meaning of baptism. He had questioned Jared about his own feelings and understanding of this special event in his life. Jared had the paper which would enable him to be baptized, and his father had the paper stating that he was qualified and willing to perform the baptism of his son, and both were signed by the bishop.

Before the family left for the chapel where the baptism would be held, Jared's father led them in a special family prayer. Jared could feel the spirit of love and warmth around him. It made him feel strong and happy inside.

There were ten children being baptized, Jared discovered. He changed from his own clothes into the white clothing he would wear and walked with his father to the place where the others were sitting. There was only time to smile at Matthew, who looked happier than Jared had ever seen him—even if he did look scared to death at the same time! Jared hoped his own fears didn't show too much.

Jared happened to sit close to Rachel. She leaned over, her eyes sparkling, and whispered, "We did it, Jared! Can you believe it?"

It *was* difficult for Jared to believe that Matthew Williams was sitting here and that he had changed so much. But then, Jared knew that Matthew wasn't the only one who had grown and changed.

In the service before the baptisms the speaker told the young people that when they came up out of the waters of baptism, it was a turning point in their lives.

"This is your day," he told them. "Your covenant, your promise. If you keep your promise to obey the commandments, Heavenly Father will keep His promise to you, and His spirit will be with you to help you always."

He demonstrated for them how the baptism would be performed, so each child would know how to hold his nose with one hand while his other hand rested on the arm of the person who was baptizing him. Jared knew how to hold his breath and how to relax in the water so all of him would

go under in the right way.

When it was Jared's turn to be baptized, he walked down into the water with his father. A warm feeling from deep inside seemed to spread all through him. He looked at his father's face and saw the deep love there. He stood in the water listening to his father's rich, strong voice speak the sacred words as he raised his right arm to the square:

"Jared Joseph Campbell, having been commissioned of
Jesus Christ, I baptize you in the name of the Father
and of the Son and of the Holy Ghost. Amen."

As his father placed his right hand on Jared's back, lightly between his shoulders, Jared thought briefly about John the Baptist baptizing Jesus in the River Jordan. Then he was slipping easily into the warm water. And, as his father raised him out again, Jared's spirit flooded with joy. His father's eyes smiled into his own for a brief moment, and Jared felt suddenly grateful for his own personal knowledge that he had just been baptized with real power and authority and that his baptism would be honored and sustained by his Father in Heaven!

Chapter Twelve

The next day, the Sabbath, was a beautiful day. A robin sang from the elm tree so loudly that Jared, up in his bedroom, could hear. There were delicate pink roses and saucy yellow daffodils growing in Sarah's garden. Even the clear sky shone a brilliant blue as if it shared in the special joy of the day.

Today Jared would receive the second part of the ordinance—the baptism of the Holy Ghost—which would confirm him a member of The Church of Jesus Christ of Latter-day Saints. Now at last his name could be recorded as an official, permanent member of the Church!

He sat in the quiet chapel beside his mother, his mind almost too full, too excited to think. His Grandpa and Grandma Campbell were here and his Grandma Davis; all his aunts and uncles and cousins, too. He wondered if Grandpa Davis could see him now and what he thought of Matthew Williams, sitting quietly beside his own grandfather, all clean in a suit and tie, getting confirmed a member of the Church.

Jared knew he would still have to help Matthew. People don't change and grow strong overnight. Matthew would need a lot of love and friendship to help him live the commandments and choose the right. But the thought didn't bother Jared. It wasn't so bad being Matthew's friend anymore. And besides, Jared had learned a secret. He had discovered that everything he did to help Matthew helped himself! He had never felt so happy as he had these past weeks when he had been thinking and working and praying for somebody else.

When the moment came, Jared walked up with his father to the front of the chapel. He sat on the chair placed especially for him. He felt the warm weight of his father's hands laid on his head. Then the hands of the bishop and his grandfather and his uncles were added. These were the hands of men he loved, men he trusted, men who held power and

56

authority from on high and were prepared to use it in Jared's behalf.

His father called him by name and then spoke some of the most beautiful words Jared had ever heard:

> "We, the Elders of Israel, lay our hands upon your head and confirm you a member of The Church of Jesus Christ of Latter-day Saints, and we say unto you, receive the Holy Ghost."

A feeling of absolute joy coursed through Jared. He felt he would remember this beautiful moment the rest of his life. He knew the Holy Ghost was a gift from Heavenly Father, and he felt both proud and humble to know that he, Jared Campbell, was willing and worthy to receive it. He wanted the Holy Ghost to be with him always, and he wanted to live so that one day he, too, would be worthy to hold the priesthood—the power to act in the name of God. What a joy it would be to bless the lives of others as his father had blessed his own life today!

The first face Jared saw when he opened his eyes was Matthew's. For a moment the two boys smiled at each other across the room, and Jared knew that perfect happiness which comes from sharing light and happiness with someone else. The glow of that happiness lighted Jared's face as he rose—his father's arm warm around him—to shake hands with the men who were waiting to welcome him into the Church, into membership in our Heavenly Father's kingdom upon the earth.